BOOK 1

Easy Classical Piano Duets

FOR TEACHER AND STUDENT

Selected and Edited by Gayle Kowalchyk and E. L. Lancaster

ABOUT THIS COLLECTION

Teachers realize the value of having their students play duets from the earliest years of piano study. Consequently, the most successful piano methods available today include teacher-student duets in the beginning levels.

The first known duets were written as early as the late 16th or early 17th century, and piano teachers have composed teacher-student duets since the 18th century. This collection contains teacher-student duets written by five teachers and composers who lived in the 18th and 19th centuries.

These duets can be used with beginning students of all ages. However, to facilitate ease in reading the score by young students, the primo and secondo parts are on separate pages. In addition, the student parts are limited to a single five-finger position, are notated in treble and bass clef, and fall mostly within the grand-staff reading range.

Arranged in approximate order of difficulty of the student part, the duets can be used for sight reading or ensemble repertoire. Students will be motivated by the full sounds that result from the added teacher part as they acquire security with tempo and rhythm provided by ensemble performance. Enjoy!

SECONDO
Student

Morning Prayer

from *18 Short Pieces*

Cornelius Gurlitt (1820–1901)
Op. 136, No. 1

Maestoso

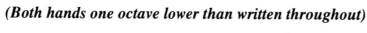

(Both hands one octave lower than written throughout)

PRIMO
Teacher

Morning Prayer

from *18 Short Pieces*

Cornelius Gurlitt (1820 –1901)
Op. 136, No. 1

Maestoso

SECONDO
Teacher

Waltz
from *Melodious Exercises*

Hermann Berens (1826 –1880)
Op. 62, No. 3

PRIMO
Student

Waltz
from *Melodious Exercises*

Hermann Berens (1826–1880)
Op. 62, No. 3

(Both hands two octaves higher than written throughout)

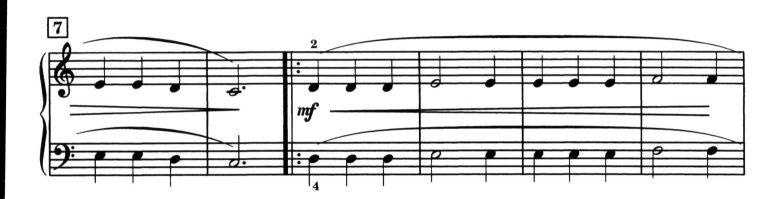

SECONDO
Teacher

Lyric Piece
from *The Children's Musical Friend*

Heinrich Wohlfahrt (1797 –1883)
Op. 87, No. 27

D. C. al Fine

Lyric Piece

PRIMO
Student

from *The Children's Musical Friend*

Heinrich Wohlfahrt (1797 –1883)
Op. 87, No. 27

(Both hands two octaves higher than written throughout)

SECONDO
Teacher

March
from *Melodious Exercises*

Hermann Berens (1826 – 1880)
Op. 62, No. 5

Allegro

PRIMO
Student

March

from *Melodious Exercises*

Hermann Berens (1826 –1880)
Op. 62, No. 5

(Both hands two octaves higher than written throughout)

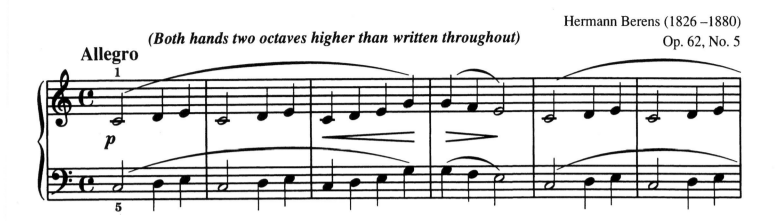

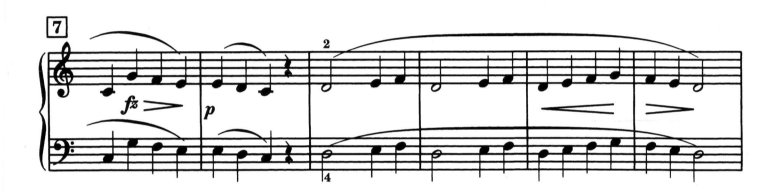

SECONDO
Teacher

Galop
from *The Children's Musical Friend*

Heinrich Wohlfahrt (1797 –1883)
Op. 87, No. 15

PRIMO
Student

Galop

from *The Children's Musical Friend*

Heinrich Wohlfahrt (1797–1883)
Op. 87, No. 15

(Both hands one octave higher than written throughout)

Allegro

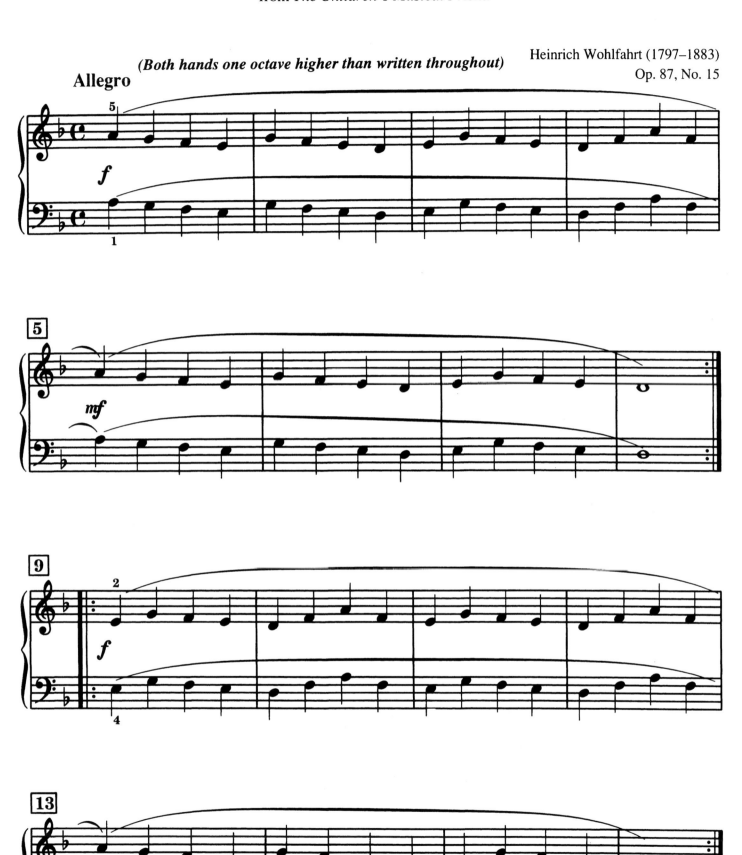

SECONDO
Student

The Contest

from *18 Short Pieces*

Cornelius Gurlitt (1820 –1901)
Op. 136, No. 3

(RH one octave lower than written throughout)

PRIMO
Teacher

The Contest

from *18 Short Pieces*

Cornelius Gurlitt (1820 –1901)
Op. 136, No. 3

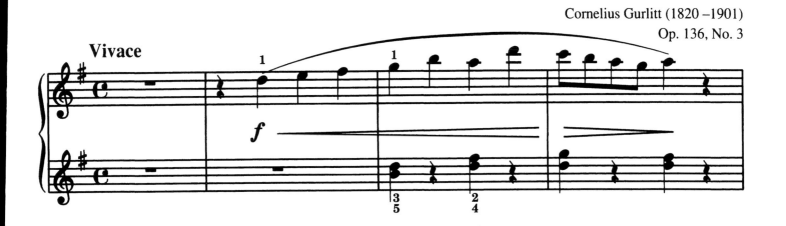

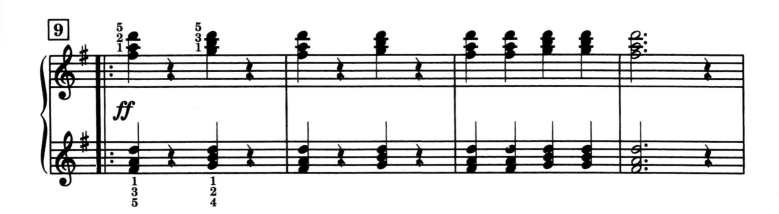

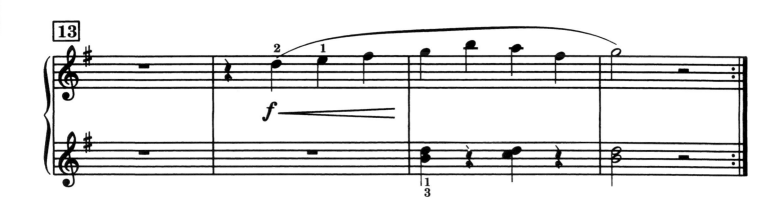

SECONDO
Student

Longing for Home
from *18 Short Pieces*

Andantino

Cornelius Gurlitt (1820 –1901)
Op. 136, No. 7

(RH two octaves lower than written throughout)

(LH one octave lower than written throughout)

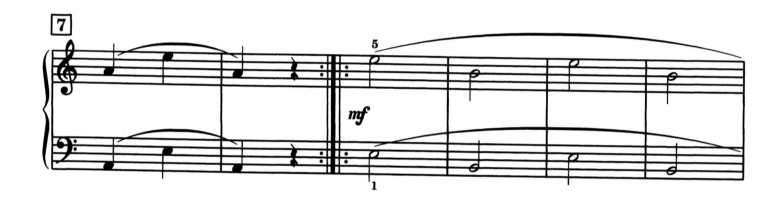

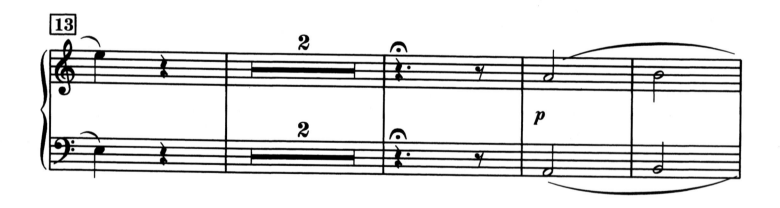

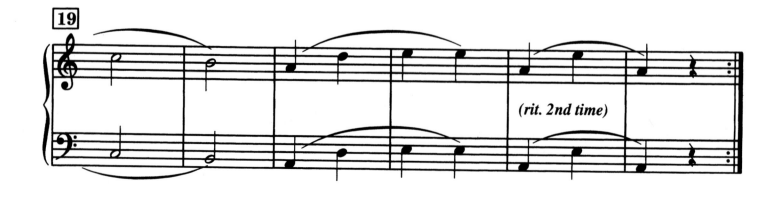

PRIMO
Teacher

Longing for Home

from *18 Short Pieces*

Cornelius Gurlitt (1820 –1901)
Op. 136, No. 7

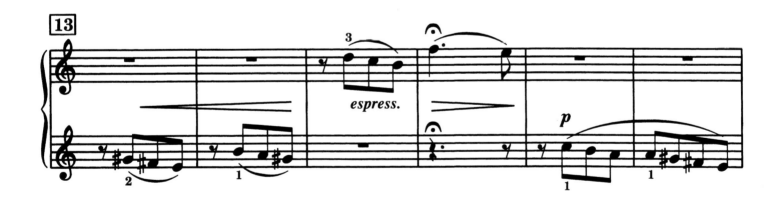

SECONDO
Teacher

Prelude

from *The Children's Musical Friend*

Heinrich Wohlfahrt (1797–1883)
Op. 87, No. 2

PRIMO
Student

Prelude

from *The Children's Musical Friend*

Heinrich Wohlfahrt (1797 –1883)
Op. 87, No. 2

Lento

(RH one octave higher than written throughout)

(LH two octaves higher than written throughout)

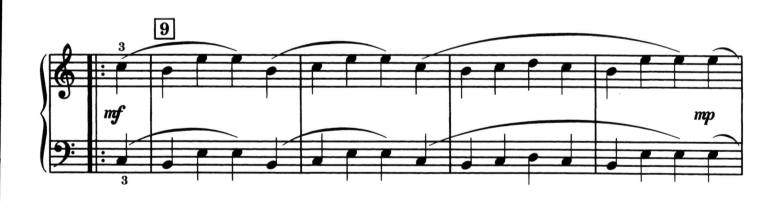

SECONDO
Teacher

Waltz

from *The Children's Musical Friend*

Heinrich Wohlfahrt (1797–1883)
Op. 87, No. 39

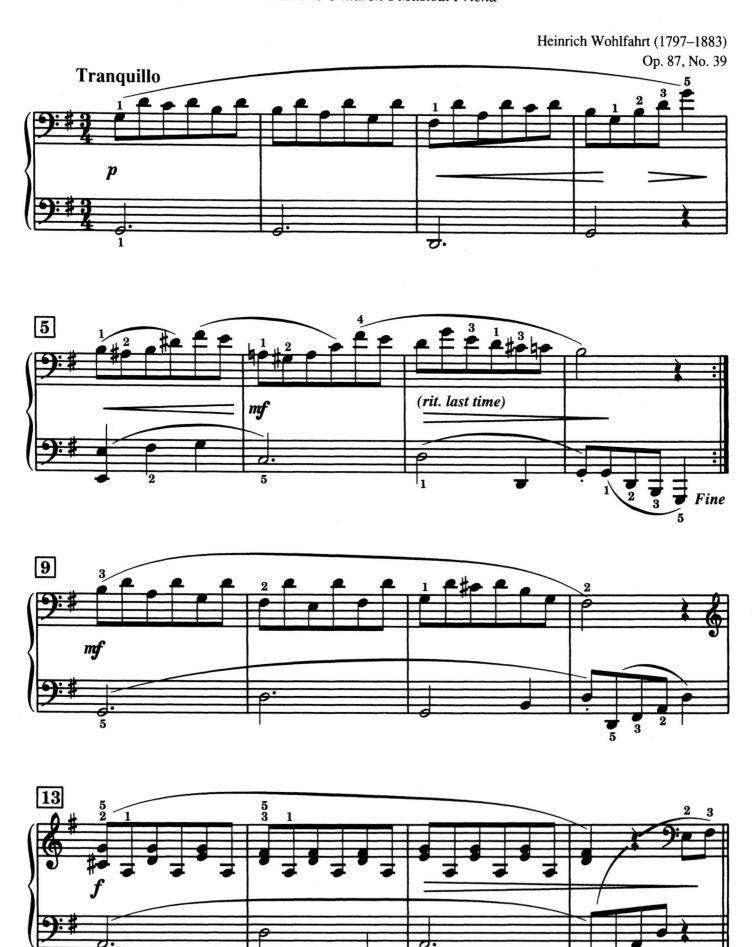

PRIMO
Student

Waltz

from *The Children's Musical Friend*

Heinrich Wohlfahrt (1797–1883)
Op. 87, No. 39

Tranquillo

(RH one octave higher than written throughout)

(LH two octaves higher than written throughout)

Fine

D. C. al Fine

SECONDO
Teacher

Waltz

from *The Children's Musical Friend*

Heinrich Wohlfahrt (1797–1883)
Op. 87, No. 35

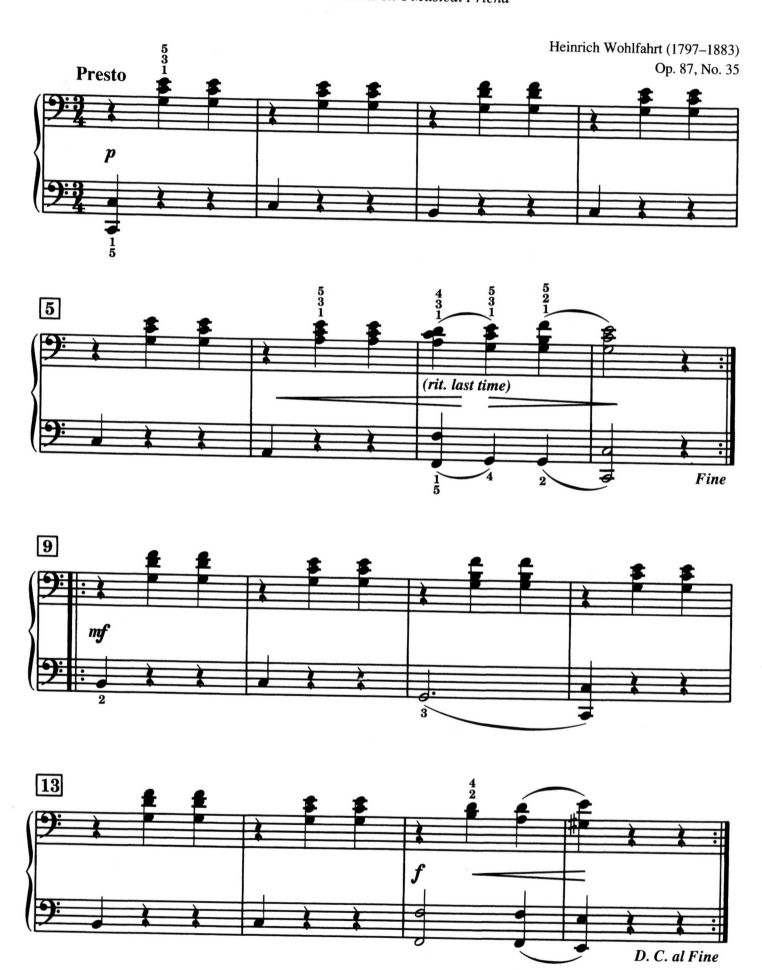

PRIMO
Student

Waltz
from *The Children's Musical Friend*

Heinrich Wohlfahrt (1797–1883)
Op. 87, No. 35

Presto *(Both hands two octaves higher than written throughout)*

Fine

D. C. al Fine

SECONDO
Teacher

March

from *Melodious Pieces*

Anton Diabelli (1781–1858)
Op. 149, No. 4

PRIMO
Student

March

from *Melodious Pieces*

Anton Diabelli (1781–1858)
Op. 149, No. 4

Allegro *(Both hands two octaves higher than written throughout)*

SECONDO
Teacher

Andantino

from *Melodious Exercises*

Hermann Berens (1826–1880)
Op. 62, No. 9

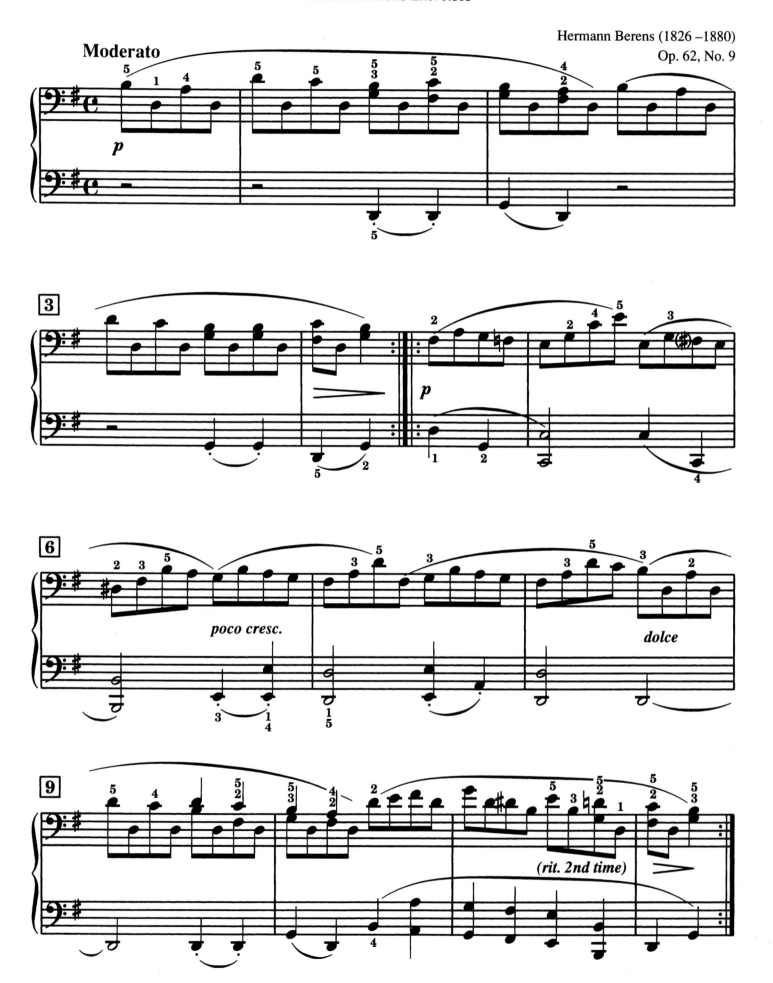

PRIMO
Student

Andantino

from *Melodious Exercises*

Hermann Berens (1826 –1880)
Op. 62, No. 9

(RH one octave higher than written throughout)

Moderato

p

(LH two octaves higher than written throughout)

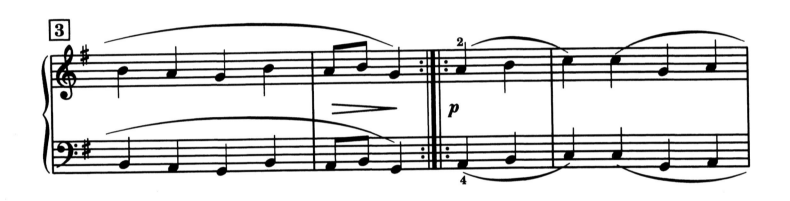

p

poco cresc.

dolce

(rit. 2nd time)

SECONDO
Teacher

Scherzo

from *Melodious Pieces*

Anton Diabelli (1781–1858)
Op. 149, No. 6

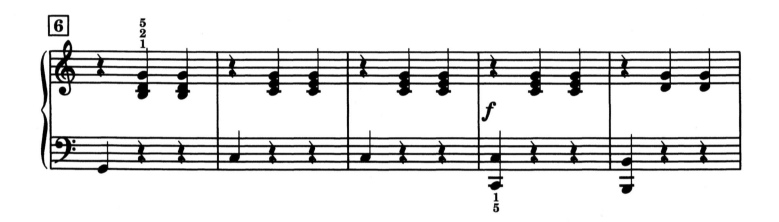

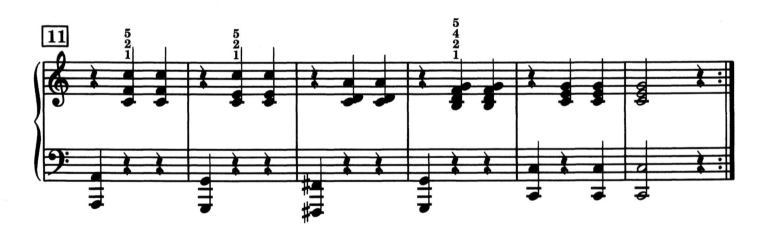

PRIMO
Student

Scherzo

from *Melodious Pieces*

Anton Diabelli (1781–1858)
Op. 149, No. 6

Allegro *(Both hands two octaves higher than written throughout)*

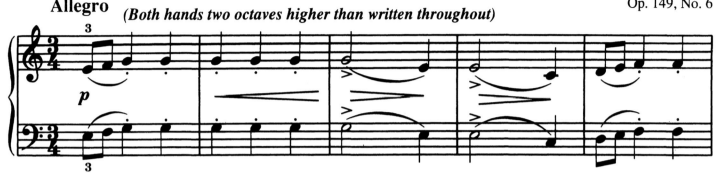

28

SECONDO (Teacher)

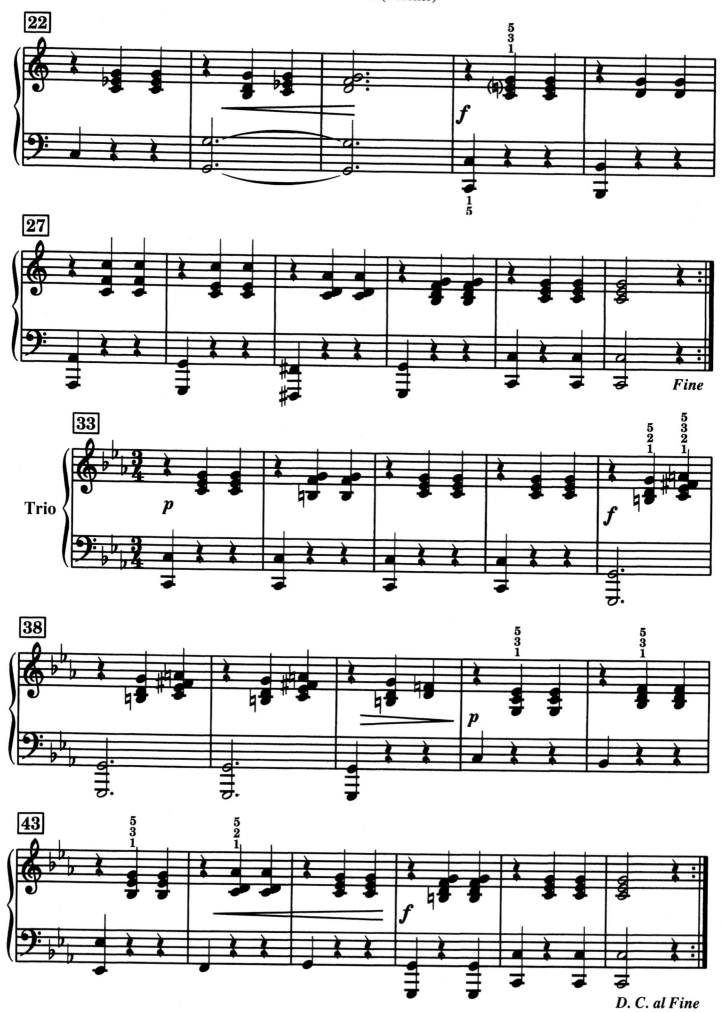

PRIMO (Student)

Fine

Trio

D. C. al Fine

SECONDO
Teacher

Waltz

from *Melodious Pieces*

Anton Diabelli (1781–1858)
Op. 149, No. 8

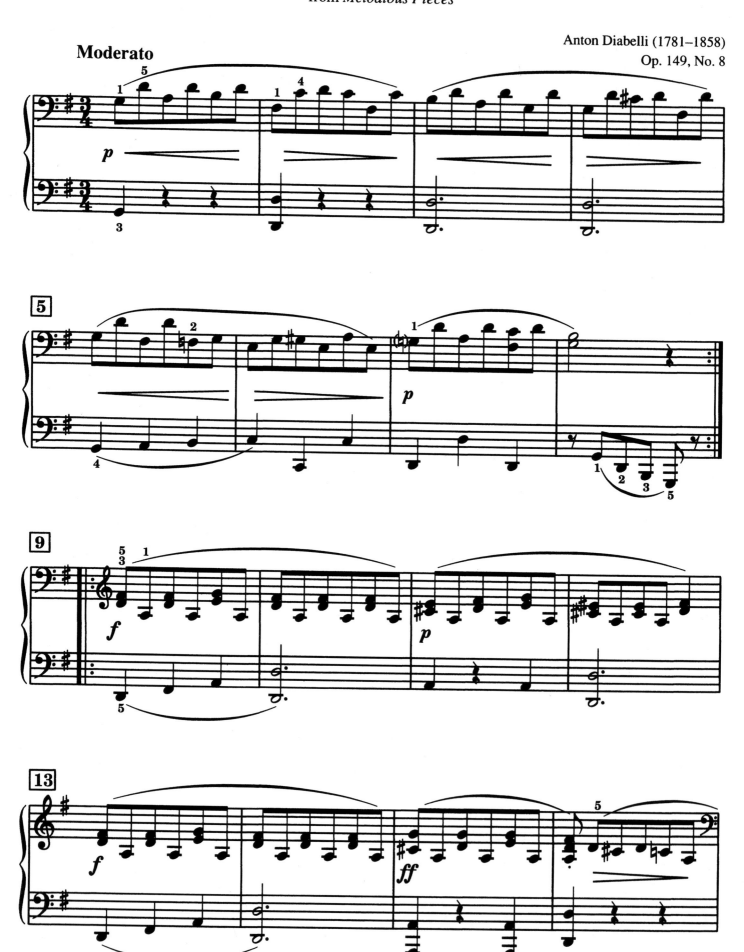

PRIMO
Student

Waltz

from *Melodious Pieces*

Anton Diabelli (1781–1858)
Op. 149, No. 8

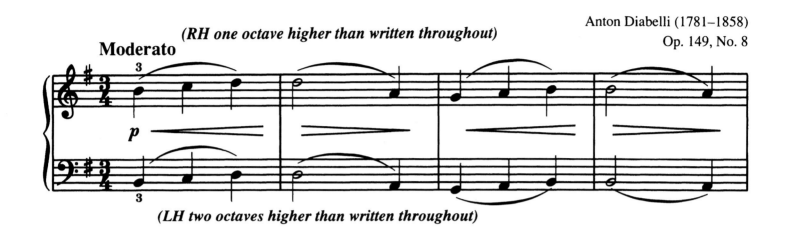

(RH one octave higher than written throughout)

Moderato

(LH two octaves higher than written throughout)

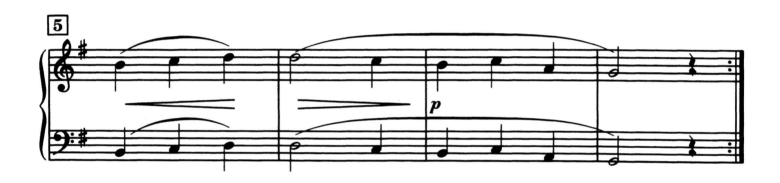

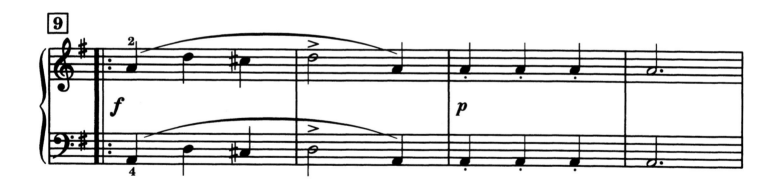

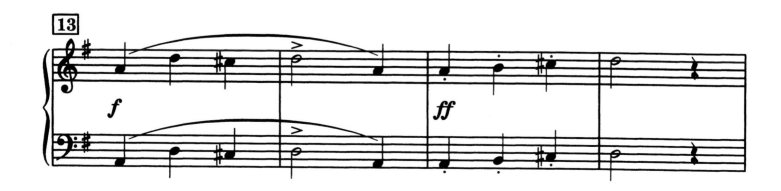

32

SECONDO (Teacher)

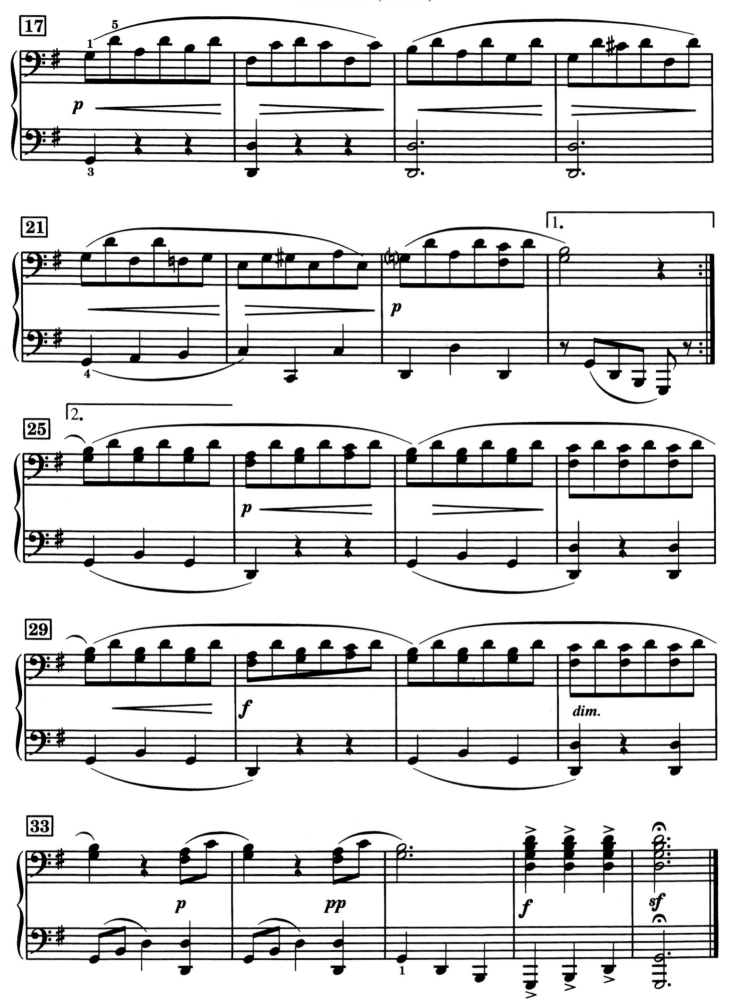

PRIMO (Student)

SECONDO
Teacher

Mazurka

from *Ingenuità*

Ernesto Becucci (1845–1905)
Op. 308, No. 3

PRIMO
Student

Mazurka

from *Ingenuità*

Ernesto Becucci (1845–1905)
Op. 308, No. 3

Moderato *(Both hands two octaves higher than written throughout)*

SECONDO (Teacher)

PRIMO (Student)

SECONDO
Teacher

Polka

from *Ingenuità*

Ernesto Becucci (1845–1905)
Op. 308, No. 2

Allegro

PRIMO
Student

Polka

from *Ingenuità*

Ernesto Becucci (1845–1905)
Op. 308, No. 2

Allegro *(Both hands two octaves higher than written throughout)*

SECONDO (Teacher)

PRIMO (Student)

SECONDO
Teacher

Waltz

from *Ingenuità*

Ernesto Becucci (1845–1905)
Op. 308, No. 1

PRIMO
Student

Waltz

from *Ingenuità*

Ernesto Becucci (1845–1905)
Op. 308, No. 1

Allegro *(Both hands two octaves higher than written throughout)*

44

PRIMO (Student)

SECONDO (Teacher)

D. S. 𝄋 al Fine

PRIMO (Student)

D. S. 𝄋 al Fine

About the Composers

Ernesto Becucci (1845–1905), an Italian, is best known for the light style and character of his piano works. He also wrote sacred music, songs and several sets of piano duets at the elementary and intermediate levels. Three of the four pieces from his set entitled *Ingenuità* are contained in this collection.

Hermann Berens (1826–1880), a German, spent most of his adult life in Sweden where he was active as a pianist in chamber music concerts in Stockholm. He was a professor at the Stockholm Conservatory and was the piano teacher of Queen Lovisa. In addition to many pieces for piano, he wrote operas, chamber music and songs.

Anton Diabelli (1781–1858), an Austrian publisher and composer, wrote numerous piano duets. He was the publisher of Schubert's first printed works. An experienced musician, piano teacher and composer, he was able to respond to the musical fashions of the time. Consequently, his publishing company was a huge financial success.

Cornelius Gurlitt (1820–1901), a German, was a member of an artistic family. Active as an organist, he wrote operas and songs as well as numerous educational piano pieces. His piano miniatures are similar in style to Schumann. Among his piano works are several piano duets.

Heinrich Wohlfahrt (1797–1883), a German, was a composer and piano teacher. He wrote a large quantity of educational piano music, including original music and arrangements. The selections in this collection are from *The Children's Musical Friend*, which contains 50 duets in progressive order.